D1609141

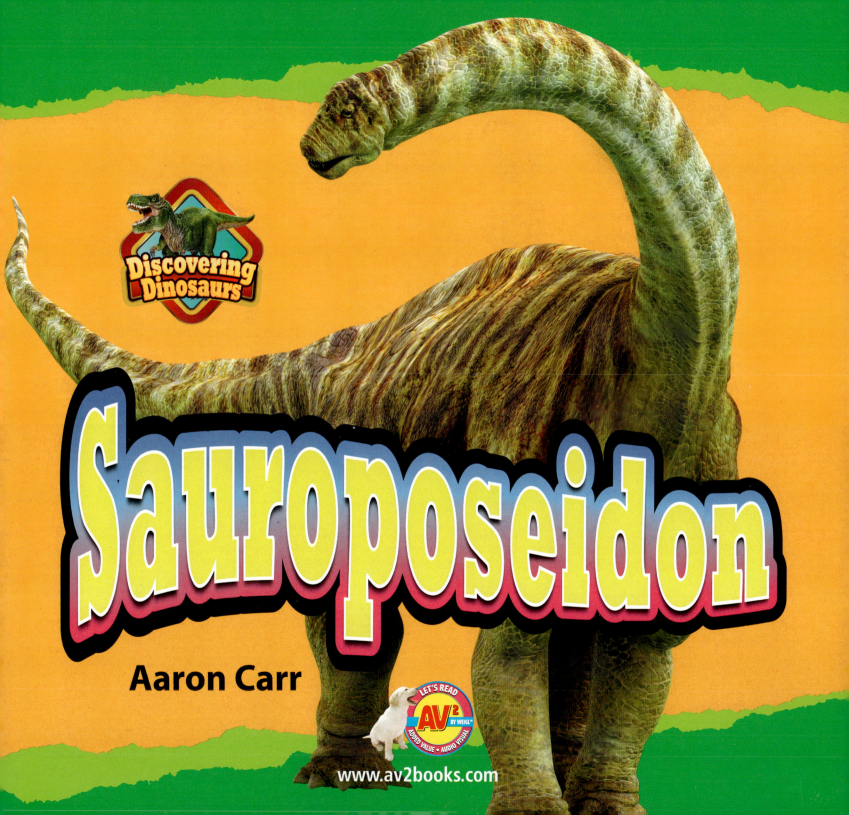

Discovering Dinosaurs

Sauroposeidon

Aaron Carr

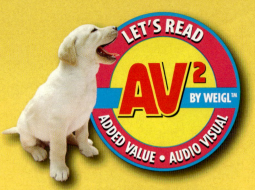

LET'S READ
AV²
BY WEIGL™
ADDED VALUE · AUDIO VISUAL

AV² provides enriched content that supplements and complements this book. Weigl's AV² books strive to create inspired learning and engage young minds in a total learning experience.

Your AV² Media Enhanced books come alive with...

Audio
Listen to sections of the book read aloud.

Video
Watch informative video clips.

Embedded Weblinks
Gain additional information for research.

Try This!
Complete activities and hands-on experiments.

Key Words
Study vocabulary, and complete a matching word activity.

Quizzes
Test your knowledge.

Slide Show
View images and captions, and prepare a presentation.

... and much, much more!

Go to **www.av2books.com**, and enter this book's unique code.

BOOK CODE

C450595

AV² by Weigl brings you media enhanced books that support active learning.

Published by AV² by Weigl
350 5th Avenue, 59th Floor
New York, NY 10118

Websites: www.av2books.com   www.weigl.com

Library of Congress Control Number: 2013953045
ISBN 978-1-4896-0592-4 (hardcover)
ISBN 978-1-4896-0593-1 (softcover)
ISBN 978-1-4896-0594-8 (multi-user eBook)
ISBN 978-1-4896-0595-5 (single-user eBook)

Printed in the United States of America in North Mankato, Minnesota
1 2 3 4 5 6 7 8 9 0   17 16 15 14 13

122013
WEP301113

Project Coordinator: Aaron Carr
Art Director: Terry Paulhus

All illustrations by Jon Hughes, pixel-shack.com.

Sauroposeidon

In this book,
you will learn

what its
name means

what it
looked like

where it lived

what it ate

and much more!

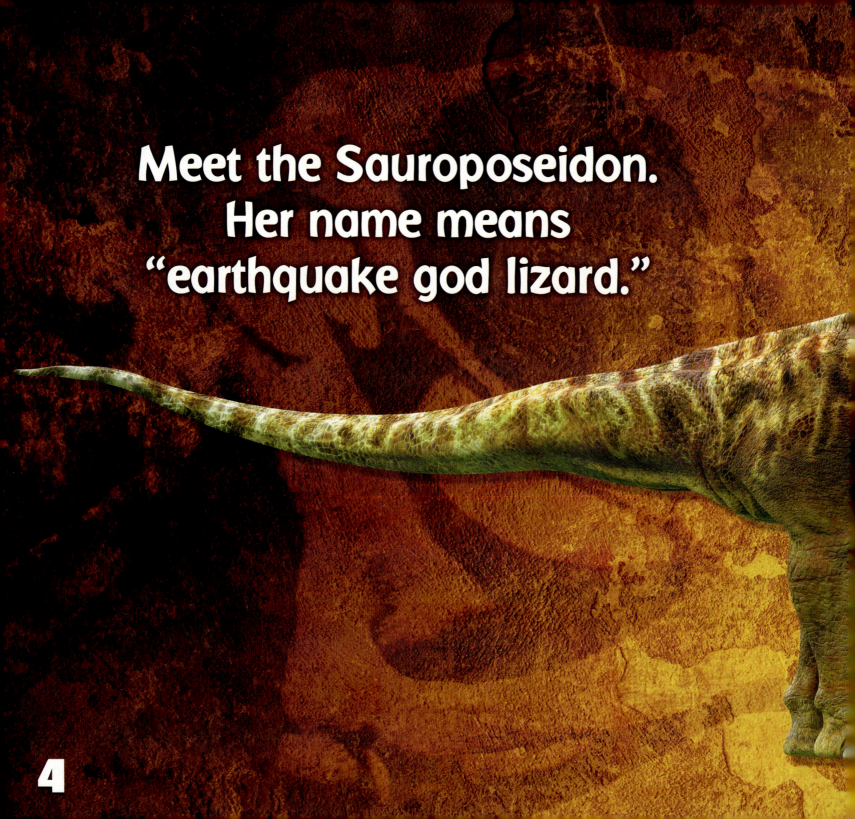

Meet the Sauroposeidon.
Her name means
"earthquake god lizard."

She was one of the largest dinosaurs ever to live.

She was as tall
as a six-floor building.

She had the longest neck
of any dinosaur.
Her neck was longer
than a school bus.

She was a plant-eater.
She may have used her long neck
to eat leaves from the tops
of tall trees.

She had to eat
a few tons of food every day.
She spent much of her time
eating or looking for food.

She walked very slowly on four huge legs.

Her legs were as big as tree trunks.

15

She lived in wooded places near water. She was found in the south part of North America.

She lived about
110 million years ago.
She was one of the last large
dinosaurs known as sauropods.

People know
about her
because of fossils.

People can go to museums to learn more about dinosaurs like Sauroposeidon.

Sauroposeidon Facts

These pages provide detailed information that expands on the interesting facts found in the book. They are intended to be used by adults as a learning support to help young readers round out their knowledge of each amazing dinosaur or pterosaur featured in the *Discovering Dinosaurs* series.

Pages 4–5

Sauroposeidon means "earthquake god lizard." Poseidon was the Greek god of Earthquakes. It was named for its sheer massive size, which scientists think may have caused the ground to shake when Sauroposeidon walked. Scientists have only known of Sauroposeidon's existence for about 20 years, so there are still a great many details about this ancient giant that people do not know. Sauroposeidon was one of the last sauropods, a group of huge, long-necked dinosaurs.

Pages 6–7

Sauroposeidon was one of the largest dinosaurs that ever lived. Scientists estimate Sauroposeidon stood about 60 feet (18 meters) tall and weighed about 65 tons (60 metric tons). Including its tail, Sauroposeidon may have measured as much as 92 feet (28 m) long. Unlike other sauropods, such as Apatosaurus, Sauroposeidon was shaped like a giraffe, with a short body, a long neck, and longer front legs than back legs. However, Sauroposeidon was up to 30 times larger than even the largest giraffe.

Pages 8–9

Sauroposeidon had the longest neck of any dinosaur. Many sauropods had long tails to counterbalance their long necks, but Sauroposeidon's neck was much longer than its tail. Its neck was about 40 feet (12 m) long. A single vertebra in Sauroposeidon's neck was up to 4 feet (1.2 m) long. Unlike many other sauropods, however, Sauroposeidon held its neck in a mostly vertical position. This may have been made possible by the light-weight construction of its vertebrae, which were made up of thin layers of bone surrounding pockets of air.

Pages 10–11

Sauroposeidon was a herbivore, or plant-eater. Though very little is known about Sauroposeidon's diet and behavior, scientists can guess based on what is known about similar dinosaurs, such as Brachiosaurus. Sauroposeidon likely used its long neck to reach tree branches high above the ground. It may have eaten conifers and flowering trees, such as magnolias, palms, and sycamores.

Sauroposeidon had to eat a few tons (metric tons) of food every day. As one of the largest herbivores that ever walked the Earth, Sauroposeidon would have spent a large part of each day looking for and eating food. However, Sauroposeidon likely swallowed its food whole, like other sauropods, which would have greatly reduced the amount of time it would have taken to gather enough food.

Sauroposeidon moved very slowly on four huge legs. Sauropods were large, slow-moving dinosaurs. The largest sauropods, called titanosaurs, held their legs in a broader stance than other sauropods, which made them even slower. The most massive titanosaurs, such as Sauroposeidon and the even heavier Argentinosaurus, could probably only walk at about 3 miles (5 kilometers) per hour. Some scientists believe Sauroposeidon may have made the Paluxy tracks, footprints almost 3 feet (1 m) wide that were found in Texas.

Sauroposeidon lived in wooded places near rivers. It lived in the southern part of North America. This area was warm and wet during the time of Sauroposeidon. Forests, deltas, bayous, and lagoons made up much of the landscape. This area was once home to many different kinds of sauropods, but by the time Sauroposeidon lived, it was one of the last of its kind in North America.

Sauroposeidon lived about 110 million years ago during the Cretaceous Period. All that people know about Sauroposeidon comes from studying fossils, bones that have been preserved in the ground for millions of years. The first Sauroposeidon fossil was found in Oklahoma in 1994. It consisted of four vertebrae bones. No complete fossil of Sauroposeidon has ever been found.

People can go to museums to see fossils and learn more about Sauroposeidon. Millions of people around the world visit museums each year to see dinosaur fossils in person. Due to the lack of complete fossils for Sauroposeidon, few museums have Sauroposeidon displays. Some museums, however, have replica displays of Sauroposeidon to show visitors, such as the Sam Noble Museum of Natural History at the University of Oklahoma.

KEY WORDS

Research has shown that as much as 65 percent of all written material published in English is made up of 300 words. These 300 words cannot be taught using pictures or learned by sounding them out. They must be recognized by sight. This book contains 54 common sight words to help young readers improve their reading fluency and comprehension. This book also teaches young readers several important content words, such as proper nouns. These words are paired with pictures to aid in learning and improve understanding.

Page	Sight Words First Appearance
4	her, means, name, the
6	live, of, one, she, to, was
7	a, as
9	any, had, long, school, than
11	eat, from, have, may, plant, trees, used
13	day, every, few, food, for, much, or, time
14	four, on, very, walked
15	big
16	found, near, part, places, water
18	about, large, last, years
19	because, know, people
20	can, go, learn, like, more

Page	Content Words First Appearance
4	earthquake, god, lizard, Sauroposeidon (pronounced: SAWR-oh-po-SIGH-don)
6	dinosaurs
7	building, floor
9	bus, neck
11	eater, leaves, tops
13	tons
14	legs
16	North America
18	sauropods
19	fossils
20	museums

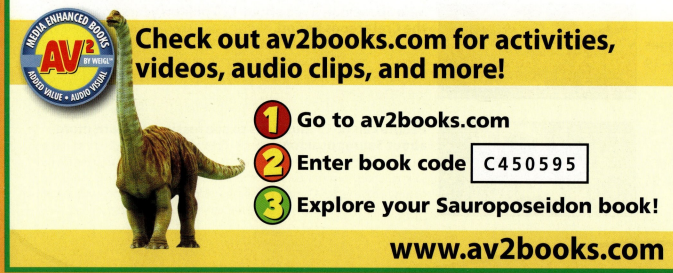